Godfrey Hall

Illustrated by Deborah Woodward

Watts Books
London • New York • Sydney

ACKNOWLEDGMENTS

The author and publishers would like to thank the following for supplying photographic material for reproduction in this book: Heather Angel p.19; Bruce Coleman Limited/Frans Lanting p.17; Bruce Coleman Limited/George Macarthy p.5; Bruce Coleman Limited/Frieder Sauer p.10; Stephen Dalton/NHPA pp.8-9, 14, 18; Ecoscene pp.2, 15; The Hutchison Library pp.7, 21; Stephen Krasemann/NHPA p.18; Swan Photographic Agency/John Buckingham pp.3, 6, 9; Swan Photographic Agency/Bill Moorcroft pp.12-13.

With thanks to the pupils and staff of Bishops Down County Primary School, Tunbridge Wells and Emily Staff.

The children on the cover are wearing clothes in the Streets Ahead range, produced exclusively for Woolworths plc by Ladybird and available in selected Woolworths stores.

Cover artwork by Gordon Monroe.

This hardback edition published 1993 by
Watts Books
96 Leonard Street
London
EC2A 4RH

Franklin Watts Australia
14 Mars Road
Lane Cove
NSW 2066

UK ISBN 0 7496 1307 6

10 9 8 7 6 5 4 3 2 1

A CIP catalogue record for this book is available from the British Library

Dewey Decimal Classification 582.16

First published in the United Kingdom in 1992 by Hodder & Stoughton Ltd

© 1992 Godfrey Hall

Printed in Great Britain by
Cambus Litho, East Kilbride

CONTENTS

Why are animals at risk?	2
Frogs and toads	4
Whale tales	6
Bat facts	8
Butterflies at risk	10
Elephants	12
Sea turtles	14
Safe homes	16
Changing ways	18
All over the world	20
Help is at hand	22
Make an elephant mask	24
Glossary and index	26

Why are animals at risk?

There are lots of endangered animals in the world. These are animals that might become **extinct** (disappear from the earth altogether).

Many of the animals are dying out because of what people are doing to the earth and the animals' environment.

Tropical rain forests are being chopped down to grow food and build roads. But at the same time, many animals' homes, or **habitats**, are being destroyed.

The dodo died out in just a few years when it was killed off by early European travellers in the seventeenth century.

Swamps and other wet places are being damaged and destroyed, killing the creatures that make their homes there. It is important that these areas do not disappear.

Some animals are killed for their skins and horns. African elephants have been killed in great numbers for their ivory tusks. Tigers have been killed for their skins.

How many endangered animals can you see on this map?

Tiger	Tree frog
Rhinoceros	African elephant
Blue Whale	Natterjack toad
Panda	Koala bear
Polar bear	Sea turtle
Fruit bat	Swallowtail butterfly

Frogs and toads

Frogs and toads like wet, damp places under stones or near water.

They spend the winter months under a stone, staying very still and safe. When the spring comes, they go back to some water, such as a pond, where they mate and lay their eggs.

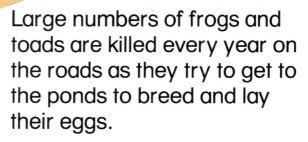

Large numbers of frogs and toads are killed every year on the roads as they try to get to the ponds to breed and lay their eggs.

In some places, people have built special underpasses beneath roads for the frogs and toads to use, or put up special signs warning drivers that frogs and toads are crossing.

It is important that frogs do not die out as they eat a lot of insects that destroy plants and crops.

Now You See

In spring, ask an adult to help you collect some frog spawn from a pond. Watch how the frog changes from an egg.

Step 1
The egg.

Step 2
Tiny tadpole.

Step 3
Baby tadpole.

Step 4
Back legs appear.

Step 5
Front legs appear.

Step 6
Small frog.

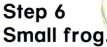

Whale tales

Whales live in the sea, and are the biggest mammals in the world. (Mammals are animals which have warm blood and feed their young on milk.) Whales have a thick layer of fat which keeps out the cold. This is called **blubber**.

This is a killer whale.

This is a sperm whale. It is the largest toothed whale and can grow up to 20 metres long. It can weigh as much as 40 tonnes.

This is a blue whale. It is the largest mammal that has ever lived.

Some whales talk to each other using lots of different sounds. Many of the sounds they make are too high or too low for us to hear. Whale songs are very beautiful to listen to.

Now You See

Collect together pictures of whales and other sea creatures. Paint a blue sea on a large piece of paper and stick the pictures on to it when it has dried.

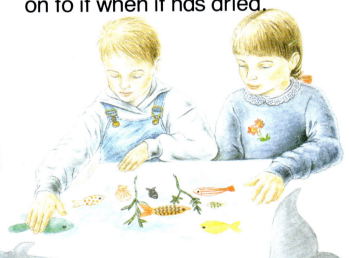

For many years, whales have been killed for their meat. Hunting by man has made them scarce. There are now rules to stop whale hunting.

AMAZING FACTS!

The baby blue whale grows from a tiny creature in its mother's inside to a creature weighing around 25 tonnes in under two years. This is the fastest rate of growth known in the animal or plant world.

Bat facts

Bats are the only mammals that are able to fly. Their wings are made of skin, not feathers.

They sleep in the daytime and come out at night. We say they are **nocturnal**.

Bats find their way at night using **echo-location**. A bat can make high-pitched squeaking sounds. These sounds bounce off objects and tell the bat what is moving in front of it and where it is. These echoes help the bat find its dinner!

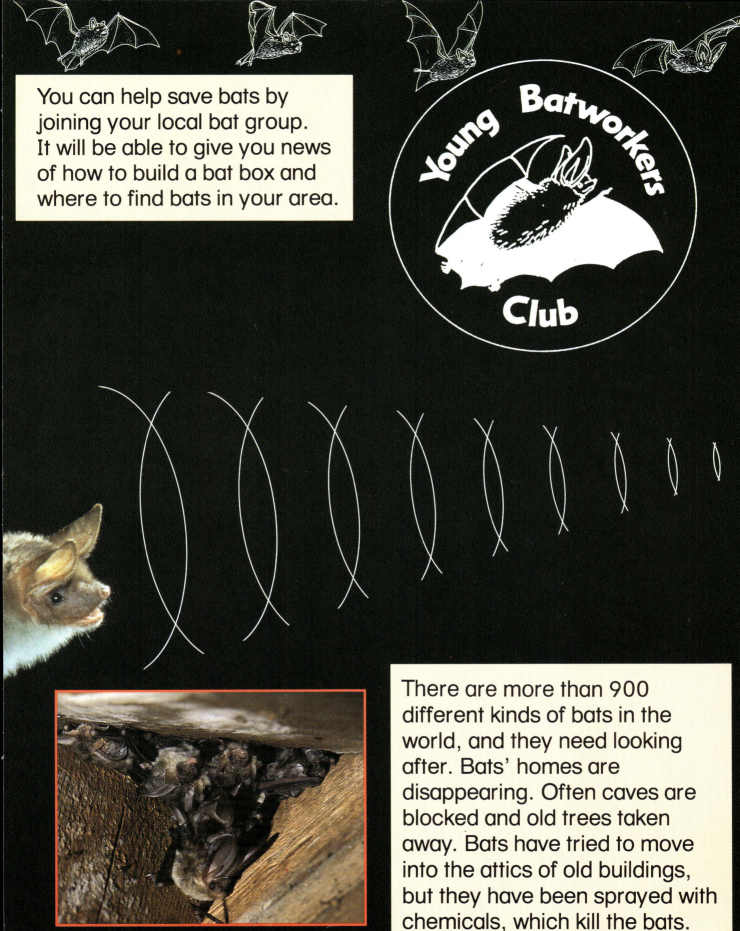

You can help save bats by joining your local bat group. It will be able to give you news of how to build a bat box and where to find bats in your area.

Young Batworkers Club

There are more than 900 different kinds of bats in the world, and they need looking after. Bats' homes are disappearing. Often caves are blocked and old trees taken away. Bats have tried to move into the attics of old buildings, but they have been sprayed with chemicals, which kill the bats.

Butterflies at risk

Chemicals are used to kill pests on crops and also help improve the way in which the plants grow. But these chemicals can poison butterflies and other small creatures that feed on the plants.

In the mountains of Mexico, special butterfly roosts have been built for the monarch butterflies which fly south for the winter from North America and Canada.

There are a number of plants we can grow in our gardens to attract butterflies, such as buddleia, lavender, candytuft and honesty.

AMAZING FACTS!

The giant birdwing butterfly of the Pacific has a wingspan of over 30 centimetres. It is often very difficult to catch butterflies as big as this as they can fly very fast.

The smallest butterfly in the world is thought to be the Dwarf Blue of Africa, which has a wingspan of 1.5 centimetres.

A number of different types of butterflies, such as the peacock and painted lady, lay their eggs on stinging nettles. These provide food and protection for the caterpillars. It is important that there are plenty of stinging nettles around in gardens and in the countryside so butterflies can lay their eggs.

Now You See

See if you can make your own butterfly print. Fold a piece of paper in half. Open it out. Put a splodge of paint on one side in the shape of a wing. Fold the paper together. Press hard and open it out carefully. You can try different colours.

Elephants

The largest land-living creature is the African elephant. Over the last 25 years, the number of African elephants that have died has increased a great deal.

This is because the land where they live is being **cultivated** (changed so it can be used for growing crops). Many elephants have been killed for their ivory tusks, which are made into ornaments and other gifts.

The poachers who kill the elephants sell the ivory in a number of different parts of the world, including Japan and the Middle East.

In Zaire in Africa, nine out of ten elephants have been killed by the poachers. If the killing goes on, by the year 2000 there will be no African elephants left.

In some countries in Africa the governments have special patrols to catch the poachers, but it can be difficult to patrol the large areas where the elephants live. Elephants are also fitted with special collars and tracked using satellites to try and prevent poachers from killing them.

You can help protect the elephants by telling your family and friends not to buy ivory objects. Write to the elephant conservation group 'Elefriends' (their address is at the back of the book) and find out what else you can do to save these animals.

Sea turtles

Sea turtles are **reptiles**. They travel thousands of miles across the sea to lay their eggs in the sand of warm, tropical beaches. Turtles nest two or three times a year, between May and September. It takes around fifty days for the eggs to hatch out. They hatch at night, and the baby turtles then have to crawl back over the sand to the sea.

Sea turtles are now endangered because, for many years, people along these coasts have been taking the turtle eggs from the sand to eat. There are now strict laws to stop this from happening, but the number of sea turtles in the world is still very small.

Even if the eggs manage to hatch, the tiny baby turtles are often taken by diving birds or fish as they struggle towards the sea.

Baby sea turtles like to eat jellyfish, and often mistake plastic bags floating in the sea for jellyfish. The plastic bags get inside their bodies and turtles may die after eating one.

At the Gumbo Limbo Nature Centre in Florida, people have been keeping a careful eye on the sea turtles. The beaches in the area are the nesting sites for hundreds of turtles.

Safe homes

It is important that we provide animals with safe places to live.

Lots of **ponds** have been filled with rubbish and chemicals which have been washed off the land. Some of the chemicals will not only kill the fish, but also small animals which drink from the pond. Chemicals can also upset the balance of the pond, using up all the oxygen in the water, preventing plants, which fish feed on, from growing.

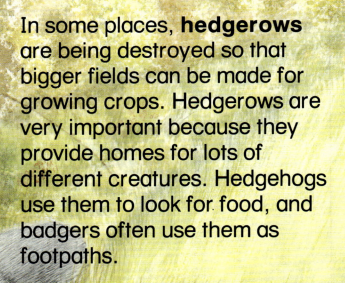

In some places, **hedgerows** are being destroyed so that bigger fields can be made for growing crops. Hedgerows are very important because they provide homes for lots of different creatures. Hedgehogs use them to look for food, and badgers often use them as footpaths.

In many parts of the world, people are opening up areas where animals can live safely, without fear of being killed or attacked by man. These are called **animal reserves**. In Kenya, there are a number of large animal reserves where visitors can see the animals in their natural homes.

AMAZING FACTS!

Over £10 million is being spent to save the Californian Condor, which is a large bird of prey. In China, twelve special reserves have been set up to look after the Giant Panda that lives in the area.

Changing ways

Some creatures have learned to survive by changing the way they live.

Foxes have moved into towns and cities in search of food. These are called **feral foxes**. They often build their dens at the bottom of gardens or in parks.

They can be seen in the early evening in back gardens and parks. They will often take food from dustbins.

The Jack Rabbit of the USA has adapted itself to desert conditions by growing large ears. These take away the heat from its body, keeping it cool.

Some creatures have learnt to blend in with the background to protect themselves. This is called **camouflage**. The Arctic Fox changes the colour of its coat to white in the winter snow.

It is important that we as people also change the way we think. In 1840 there were about 30 million bison in the USA. A century ago, there were only 1,000: the rest had been killed. Numbers have now gone up to over 30,000, because bison became protected by law.

Now You See

Get together with some friends and draw some posters telling people how they can help save our wildlife. Display your posters where other people can see them.

All over the world

Parks and special sanctuaries are being opened up around the world to help protect our wildlife.

In some places, it has been found that a way of helping protect the wildlife is to only allow a certain number of people into the park at one time.

National parks can be found in many countries such as the USA, England, Nigeria and Switzerland. The first national park to be opened in the world was Yellowstone Park in the USA. It was started in the 1870s. Many of these parks have special footpaths to stop people treading on the wild flowers and disturbing the animals.

There are a number of **Wildlife sanctuaries** in different parts of the world. Often animals in danger of extinction are kept in centres, where they breed in captivity, and are then released into the wild. One such centre is the Otter Trust in Norfolk; another is Howletts Zoo in Kent, where gorillas are bred.

Large areas of the **rain forests** are being cut down to make way for cattle breeding grounds. It is important that we control the number of trees being chopped down, and set aside reserves where the animals of the rain forests can live.

Help is at hand

How can **you** help animals at risk?

There are lots of different wildlife groups which you can join. You can write to them at the addresses below. Remember to include a stamped addressed envelope. Why not start a group of your own with some friends to help wildlife in your area?

Watch

Watch works to save the countryside and help protect wildlife. The address is:

22, The Green, Nettleham, Lincoln LN2 2NR

The Go Wild Club, Worldwide Fund for Nature

The Go Wild Club is the WWF's young people's club, offering a fun-packed factfile and lots of information on the environment. The address is:

Go Wild Club, PO Box 101, Wetherby, Yorkshire LS23 7EE

The Whale and Dolphin Conservation Society

This society works to save whales and dolphins from being hunted and killed. The address is:

20, West Lea Road, Weston, Bath BA1 3RL

Earth Action

This is the young people's section of Friends of the Earth, which encourages people to take action on a wide range of important issues on the environment. The address of both groups is:

26-28, Underwood Street, London N1 7JQ

Elefriends

Elefriends works to protect the elephants, particularly against the ivory trade.
The address is:

Cherry Tree Cottage, Coldharbour, Near Dorking, Surrey RH5 6HA

Find a piece of ground at home or at school and make it into your own wildlife park. Make sure you plant seeds that will encourage butterflies and small creatures.

Make an elephant mask

1. Trace the pieces of the mask on to some card. Remember to trace the dotted lines as well. Colour the pieces and cut them out.

2. Carefully cut round the eye holes. Make five slits in the head piece in the places marked with a dotted line.

3. Thread the trunk and tusks from behind through the slits at the bottom of the head. Slot the ears from the front into the two slits at the top of the head. Attach some elastic or string to the tabs on each side of the head. Now you're ready to wear your mask!

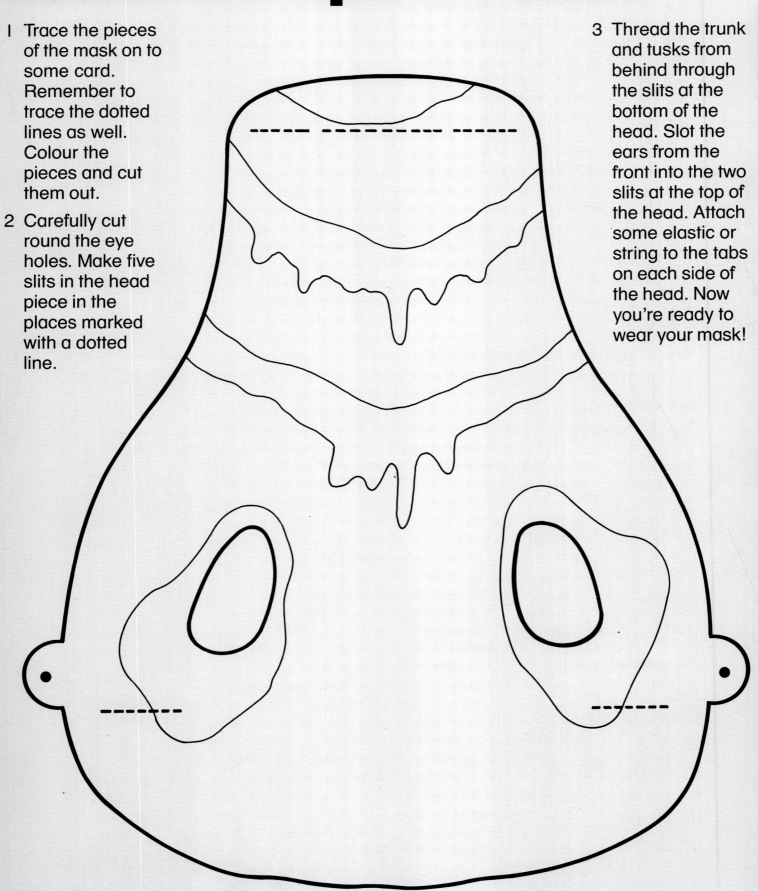

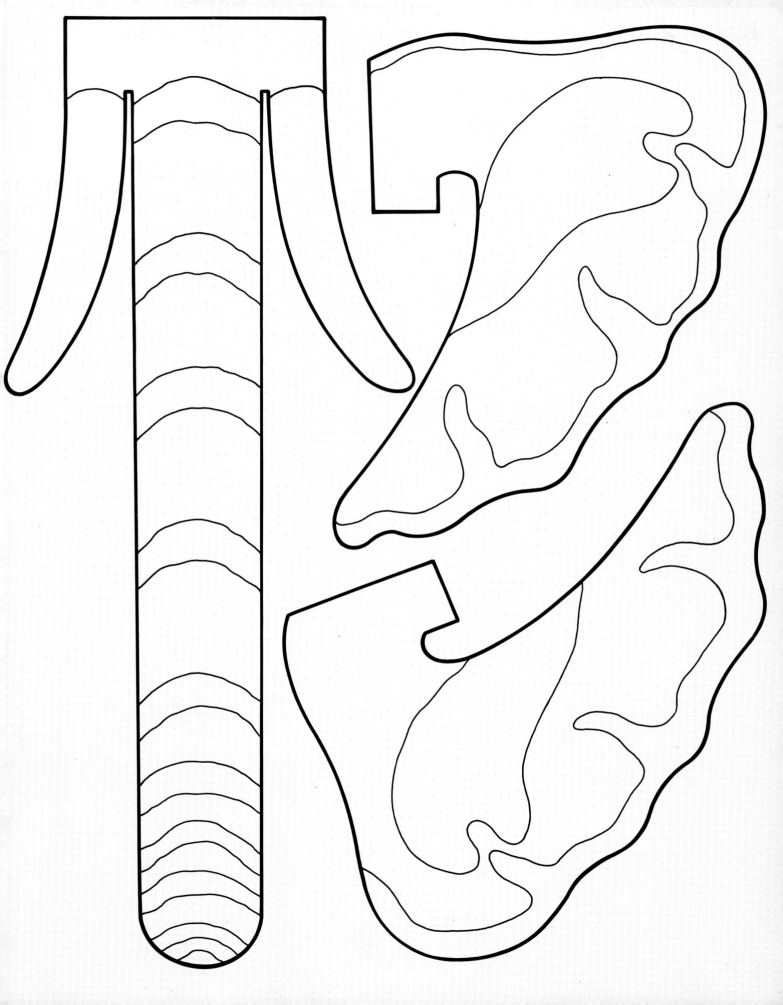

GLOSSARY

chemical Something which is sprayed on to fields to make plants grow. Chemicals are also used to kill pests and weeds.

desert A very hot, sandy part of the world where there are very few animals or plants.

dodo A flightless bird that became extinct in 1681.

frog spawn Frogs' eggs. The spawn looks like black dots in jelly.

jellyfish An animal that lives in the sea. It has a jelly-like body and long, trailing parts.

poachers People who hunt animals without permission on private land or water, often for their skin or tusks.

rain forest A thick forest in a warm, wet part of the world. Rain forests are homes to many types of plants and animals.

sanctuaries Places where animals can live safely. More and more sanctuaries are opening up around the world to protect creatures at risk.

INDEX

animal reserves 17
Arctic fox 19

bats 8-9
birdwing butterfly 11
bison 19
blue whale 6
blubber 6
butterflies 10-11

Californian Condor 17
camouflage 18-19

dodo 3
Dwarf Blue butterfly 11

elephant 3, 12-13
echo-location 8

feral fox 18
frog 4-5
frogspawn 5

Gumbo Limbo
 Nature Centre 15
Giant Panda 17

hunting 7
hedgerows 16

ivory 13

Jack Rabbit 18

killer whale 6

nettles 11
National Parks 20

painted lady butterfly 11
peacock butterfly 11
poachers 12-13
ponds 16

rain forest 2, 21

sea turtles 14-15
sperm whale 6
swamps 3

toad 4-5
tusks 12

whales 6-7
whale songs 7
wildlife sanctuaries 21